CONTENTS

Body Language	2
Faces	6
Hands & Fingers	10
Arms	13
Legs	14
People Watching	16
Signals	18
Hidden Meanings	20
Don't Get Caught	22
Eyes on You!	24

A Read-about

BODY LANGUAGE

Every time you point your finger, or stamp your foot, or stick out your tongue, you are using a special kind of language. It's a language you don't have to learn. It's a language you don't have to speak. It's a language that uses many parts of the body. That's why it's called BODY LANGUAGE.

Everyone uses body language all the time. If you know what to look for, you can often tell what others are thinking.

Sometimes it's easy. You can see that your friends are happy, or sad, or angry, even if they don't speak. Their body language tells you.

At other times the signs aren't so easy to understand. For instance, if someone talks to you with his hand over his mouth, it could be that he isn't telling the truth!

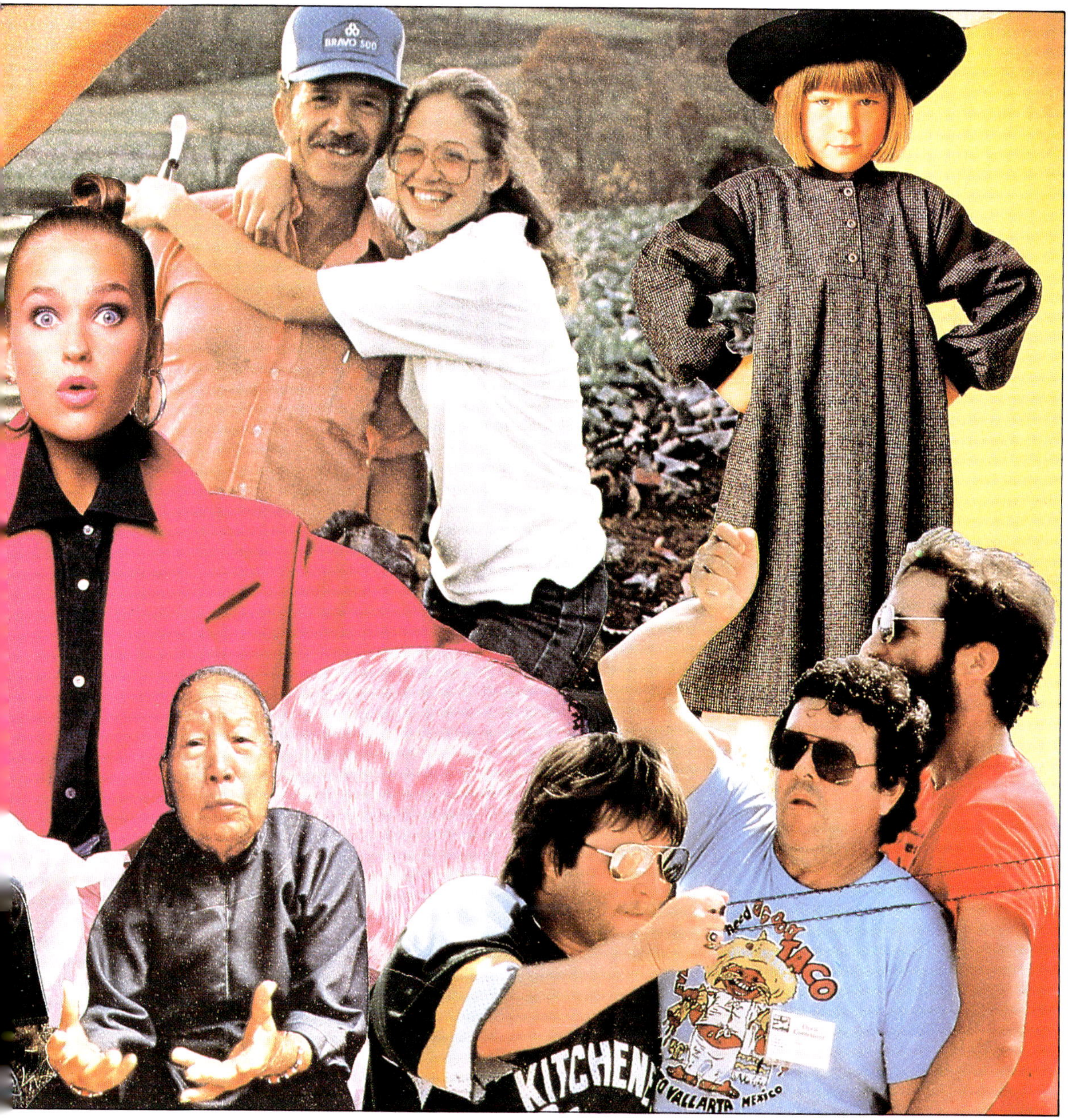
BRAVO 500
TACO
KITCHENE
VALLARTA
MEXICO

To understand body language, you have to study people. Look at them in the street, at home, and at school. Study your family, your friends, even strangers.

Notice their expressions, how they walk, what they do with their hands and their feet. From their appearance, try to sense what kind of people they are, what they might be thinking, and how they are feeling.

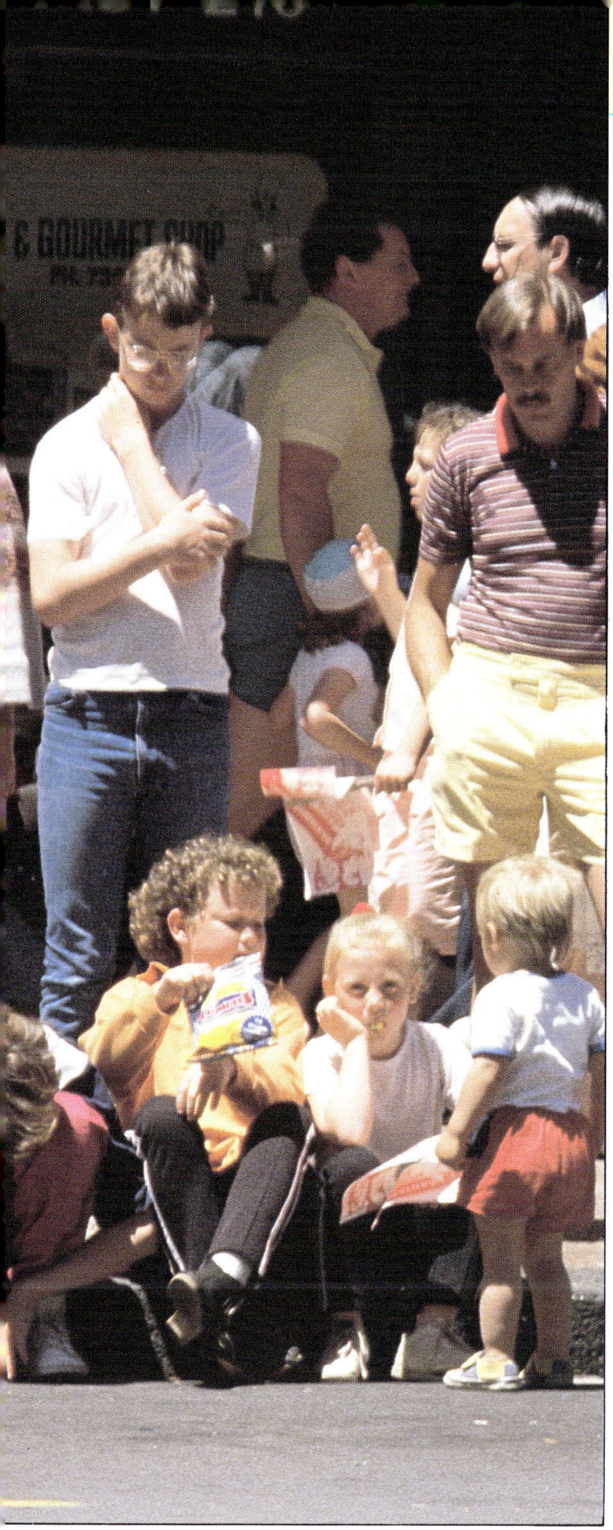
& GOURMET SHOP

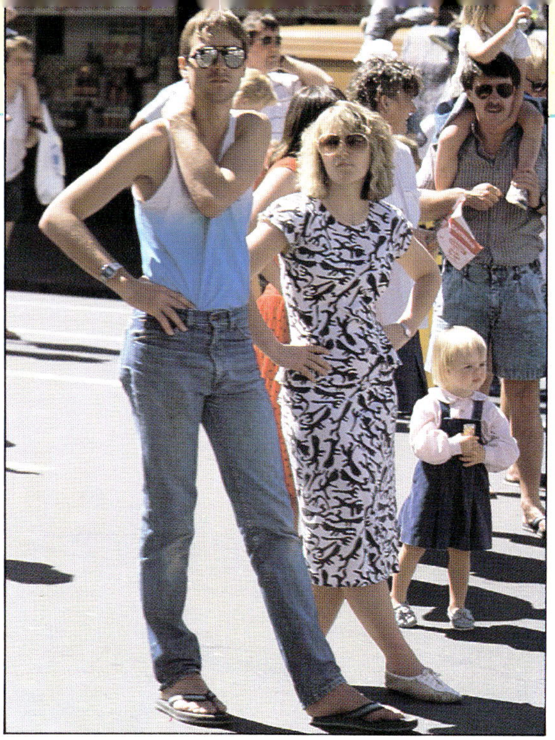

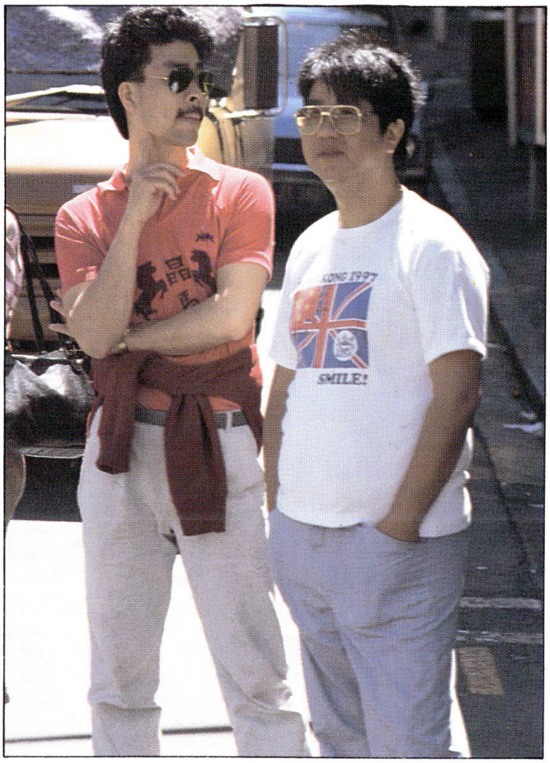
SMILE!

FACES

In body language, the face tells us more than any other part of the body. Let's examine parts of the face beginning with the eyes.

Even if you saw nothing but the eyes, you could still tell quite a lot about a person. Eyes give definite clues to someone's thoughts and feelings.

Look at the pupils first. They can change size quickly. They can grow large, or get quite small, depending on how a person is feeling. Anger, frustration, nervousness, and other negative moods make the pupils like small, hard dots. We talk about "cold eyes" or "beady eyes." When we feel excited, warm, or loving, the pupils dilate, becoming up to four times larger.

Of course, light can affect them too. In bright sunlight, the pupils get very small. In darker conditions, they become larger.

Our eyes also change shape continually. When we are really interested, they get larger, and the gaze is steady. If we're bored, the lids usually come down a little and we look away. Fright makes us wide-eyed. If a person is lying, the lids are often hooded and the eyes dart about. We say someone has "shifty eyes."

The eyebrows play a big part in the overall look of the eyes. They're like picture frames, except that they also move a lot. They can express surprise, worry, happiness, anxiety, or sadness. Sometimes just one eyebrow moves, as in asking a silent question.

When you're looking at someone eye-to-eye, you can learn a lot about the person you're looking at, so the gaze is important too. Someone who can't hold your gaze and looks down or away could be nervous, or perhaps not completely trustworthy. However, in some countries, it is not considered polite to gaze directly at another person.

If someone is hostile to you, the look in the eyes will be cold and unflinching. If the person likes you, the eyes will be warm and friendly and will look at you directly.

7

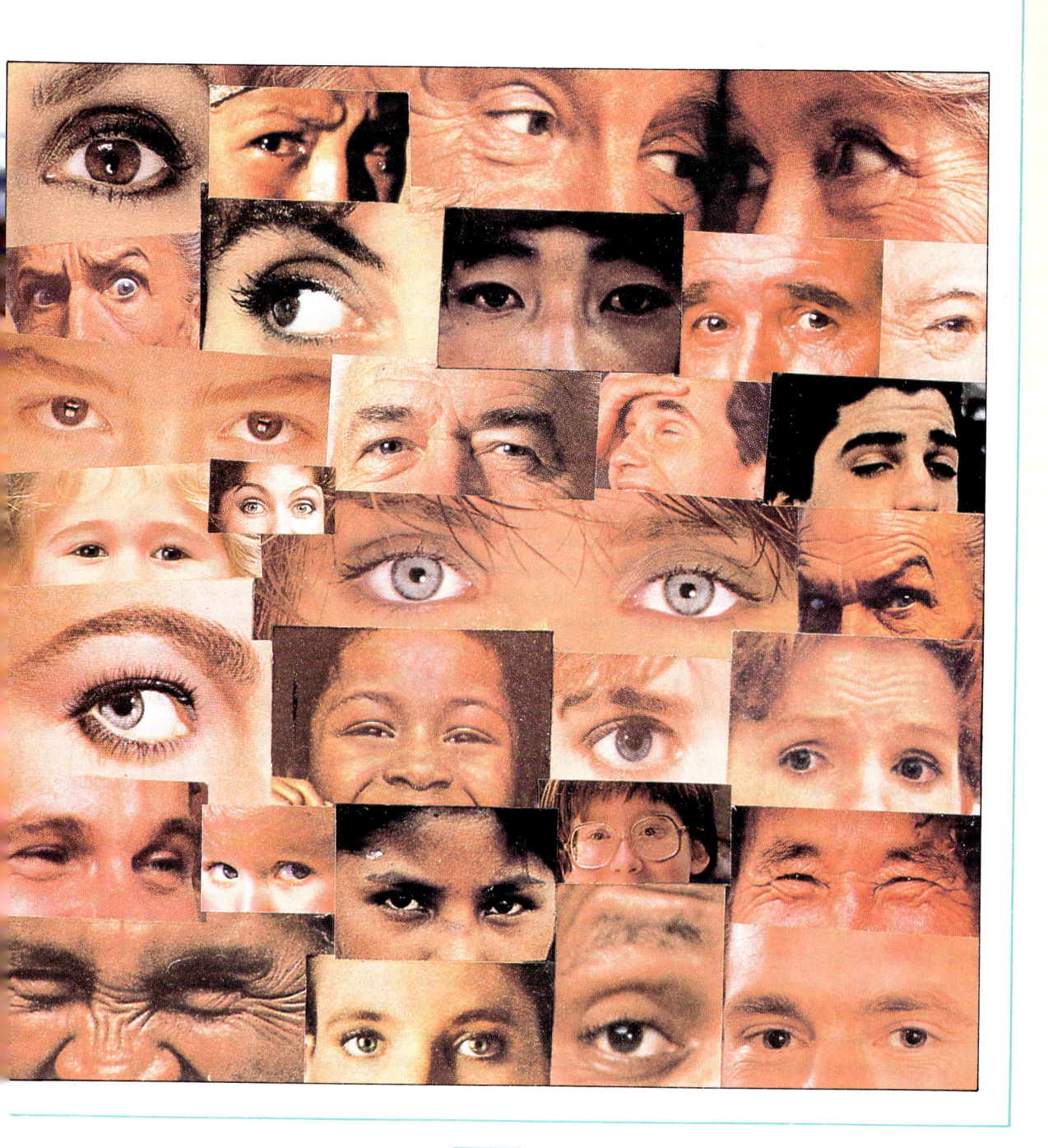

A mouth doesn't necessarily have to speak. Combined with the eyes, the mouth can also tell what a person is feeling.

Look at the pictures—which ones show that the person is amused, pleased, surprised, happy, sad, worried, shocked, horrified, relaxed, questioning?

You may think it strange that the nose is included in body language, for it doesn't do much by itself except sniff (with disapproval) and wrinkle up (in disgust). Yet the nose is really quite important.

We talk about someone putting their nose in the air, meaning she's proud; or looking down her nose, which is a good description of a critical person.

Touching the nose also gives us several signals. We hold our noses over something unpleasant and thumb our noses in defiance. Some people touch the side of the nose when they're being deceitful. Others rub the bottom of the nose when they're nervous or under stress.

9

HANDS & FINGERS

We "talk" a lot with our hands and fingers. We wave them and wiggle them. We clench them and clap them. We point and press them. And all the time we're sending out messages.

When we don't want to hear, we cover our ears with our hands. When we're distressed, we cover our faces with our hands.

When we enjoy something, we clap. When we're excited, we rub our hands together.

When we're sincere, we turn our palms towards our bodies. To calm a situation, we bring our hands downward.

An angry person's hand becomes a fist. Some people bite their nails when they're scared or wring their hands when they're anxious.

When we're thinking, sometimes we put a finger on our cheek. To make a point, we wag a finger.

When we're uncertain, we shrug with palms upward. When we're nervous, we move our fingers a lot, or perhaps twist a ring or a lock of hair.

We raise our hands in alarm or protest. When we're glad to see someone, we wave.

When we're not being truthful, we might put a finger to an eye, put one hand or finger over the mouth, or put both hands over the mouth.

Did you know...

Animals use body language too—that's how they talk to each other. We can understand some of it. For instance, all cats, from your pet to a tiger, purr when they're contented, but flatten their ears and swing their tails when they're angry. If you watch your cat when it's angry, it will puff out its fur, arch its back, and spit as well!

Dogs bare their teeth as a warning not to come closer, and their hackles rise on their backs when they're afraid or anxious. They wag their tails when they're pleased to see you. It's their way of smiling.

When a chimpanzee smiles, it is not being friendly, but is showing fear.

ARMS

Arms also play a part in body language. Crossing the arms creates a barrier. It warns people not to come closer, or it indicates aggression.

If the hands are further up the arms, however, the person could be feeling miserable and hugging himself, or perhaps he is cold!

Open arms mean just the opposite. They are welcoming. In fact, we say, "to welcome someone with open arms."

Another expression is "to keep someone at arm's length." This gesture means "keep away!"

Arms behind the back usually mean that the person is confident, because she is not afraid to expose her front, which is the most vulnerable part of the body.

13

LEGS

Most of us look at faces and don't realize how much we can learn by looking at feet and legs. You'd think that legs were just legs, but they also give out signals. Busy legs—dancing, skipping, hopping, running, jogging, walking—are obvious. We learn more when people are standing still or sitting down.

Restless and nervous people move their legs a lot, especially when they are sitting. Swinging legs show that the person is anxious to get away. Legs tightly wrapped around each other show tension, especially when they are wrapped and unwrapped. Tapping, flapping, twisting, or circling a foot shows that a person is not relaxed or at ease.

People who are relaxed generally keep their legs and feet reasonably still. A relaxed person often tucks one leg right up under the other when sitting, whereas a more cautious one might cross the legs at the knees and keep them tightly together. When someone is interested, the legs can be apart, perhaps just crossed at the ankles.

People cross their legs when standing too. This looks as though they're not quite at ease. An assertive person often stands very straight with the legs firmly apart.

PEOPLE WATCHING

It's fun to watch people in a social situation. Study each person's body language and note how people relate to each other. You will see that the space between people differs according to how well they know each other. What can you learn from the body language of the people in this picture?

16

17

SIGNALS

The body can send out many messages at the same time—literally from head to foot. To read body language well, we have to understand these signals—not one at a time, but as they occur together, in groups or clusters. Understanding them helps us to relate better to our friends, parents, teachers, and other people with whom we come in contact.

A lonely person shows negative signals and therefore does not attract people. The head drops, the eyes are downcast, and the arms may hug the body for comfort. The hands move nervously, the legs are close together, and the whole body is tense.

The young man in the top picture is rather arrogant. He is trying to make an impression as a tough guy. His head is high; his chin juts out. He expands his chest and walks with a swagger. His thumbs are thrust into his belt with his fingers pointing downward, a symbol of dominance.

This is a show-off. Casually slumped on a car, he throws his legs into an exaggerated position. His hands are behind his head. His eyelids are half down, and his attitude is one of superiority.

A "couldn't-care-less" attitude helps this girl to escape from an embarrassing or unwanted situation. She tilts her head and lifts one shoulder, twisting at the waist as she moves. She gives a little kick with her foot.

In the lower picture, the girl is interested and alert. She leans forward. Her face is lively, and her eyes are bright. Her hands are expressive. Her feet are flat on the floor, and she doesn't fidget. She will smile and nod as she listens. The situation must be difficult for the boy, however. He is tense all over. His face is tight, and his eyes stare. He is holding the arms of the chair firmly, and his legs are rigid.

HIDDEN MEANINGS

Sometimes people *say* one thing, but their body language tells you another. If there's a conflict, it's fairly safe to assume that their body language is telling the truth. Their real feelings are hard to hide.

Someone may talk of honesty, but if he's touching his face, his body language says the opposite.

If someone gives you a present you don't like, you may smile and say, "It's beautiful." To be polite, you tell a white lie, but perhaps you'll cross your fingers to protect yourself from the consequences. Also your eyes and smile will not show real pleasure.

"Of course, I didn't expect to win…" your friend may say. But chances are, she did; and she is very disappointed. She will smile for the public, but her body language—slouched shoulders and drooping head—will express sadness.

You may say you are interested in what someone is saying, but your body language may say you are bored. A drooping mouth, a body sloping back from the speaker, and crossed ankles show lack of interest.

More difficult to unravel is a conflict of body language itself—where some signs give one message and others tell a different story.

If the eyes are cold and hard—the smile could be false, especially if it's turned on and off quickly.

Laughing at a joke you don't understand creates a conflict of body language and looks forced.

People often try to appear happy even though they are very nervous. It could be their legs that give them away.

The young man in the middle picture seems to be interested, but his toe-tapping shows that he is impatient and anxious to get away.

The girl, below, wants to look serious, but by her eyes and shaking body you know she is trying not to laugh.

DON'T GET CAUGHT

Misunderstandings in body language can occur when people of different cultures get together. What is considered polite in one culture can be considered rude in another.

The body language in this book is basically for English-speaking countries, so here are just a few examples of body language in other parts of the world.

TAKE THE "CIRCLE SIGN"

In America and England, it means "AOK"—great!

In France it means zero or "worthless."

But in Japan, it's a sign for money.

When we call "come here," we beckon with the palm up and by moving the fingers towards the chin. In some countries, however, it is done with the palm downwards and the fingers pointing towards the chest. These countries include Samoa, Tunisia, Italy, and Spain.

In Pacific Island countries, it's considered very impolite to stare. Children are taught to avert their gaze and not look at someone directly.

In Arab and some Eastern countries, people stand close together, whereas we like more space around us unless we know each other very well. Westerners are sometimes offended by others invading their spaces; yet to Arabs it is not polite to stand at a distance.

Bowing is still seen in many countries. It's more than courtesy; it's a form of submissive behavior. In Polynesia, it's a mark of respect to sit or even squat.

To Westerners, shrugging the shoulders often means "I don't care," but to some people, including New Zealand Maoris, it means "I don't know," a quite different statement.

When visiting other countries, take care that your body language doesn't give offense.

EYES ON YOU!

Body language is natural to all of us. We can't *not* use it. But we can *improve* it.

If you usually sit, stand, and walk with your head down, your shoulders hunched, and your body tense, you'll always be regarded as a nervous, rather negative person. If you improve your posture and look happier, you'll feel better and your body language will be much more positive.

It's very easy to slip into poor habits, and it takes a real effort to lose them. But we are judged by how we look and react.

Understanding body language goes further than being able to interpret other people's thoughts and feelings. It can actually help you to get along better with others.

The study of body language never ends.

There's always something new to discover. Every person has a different blend of signals. That's what makes it so interesting.

When you're studying people, just remember one thing. While you're looking at *them*... they'll be looking at *you*!